TAYLOR SWIFT'S SONGWRITING

LOVE, POETRY, AND ADDRESSING THE HATERS

EVERYTHING TAYLOR SWIFT

(Gareth's Version)

BY KRISTEN RAJCZAK NELSON

Gareth Stevens PUBLISHING

Please visit our website, www.garethstevens.com. For a free color catalog of all our high-quality books, call toll free 1-800-542-2595 or fax 1-877-542-2596.

Library of Congress Cataloging-in-Publication Data
Names: Rajczak Nelson, Kristen, author.
Title: Taylor Swift's songwriting : love, poetry, and addressing the haters / Kristen Rajczak Nelson.
Description: Buffalo, NY : Gareth Stevens Publishing, 2025. | Series: Everything Taylor Swift (Gareth's version) | Includes index.
Identifiers: LCCN 2024025710 | ISBN 9781482469486 (library binding) | ISBN 9781482469479 (paperback) | ISBN 9781482469493 (ebook)
Subjects: LCSH: Swift, Taylor, 1989—Juvenile literature. | Popular music–Writing and publishing–Juvenile literature.
Classification: LCC ML3930.S989 R37 2025 | DDC 782.421642092–dc23/eng/20240611
LC record available at https://lccn.loc.gov/2024025710

Published in 2025 by
Gareth Stevens Publishing
2544 Clinton Street
Buffalo, NY 14224

Designer: Tanya Dellaccio Keeney
Editor: Kristen Nelson

Photo credits: Cover, page numbers (friendship bracelet) Yuliqwiart/Shutterstock.com; cover Brian Friedman/Shutterstock.com; p. 5 TT News Agency/Alamy Images; p. 7 (Liz Rose) MediaPunch Inc/Alamy Images; p. 7 (Taylor Swift) Courtesy of Gilles Dufresne/Flickr.com; p. 9 Debby Wong/Shutterstock.com; pp. 11 (bottom), 15 Courtesy of Paolo Villanueva/Flickr.com; p. 9 (top) https://upload.wikimedia.org/wikipedia/commons/c/ca/Taylor_Swift_RED_Tour_%288642419792%29.jpg; p. 17 (top) ASSOCIATED PRESS/AP Images; p. 17 (bottom) Hazel Player/Shutterstock.com; p. 19 a katz/Shutterstock.com; p. 21 Tinseltown/Shutterstock.com; pp. 23 (top), 27 Catrina Haze/Shutterstock.com; p. 24 (bottom) https://upload.wikimedia.org/wikipedia/commons/e/ee/Taylor_Swift_Eras_Tour_-_Arlington%2C_TX_-_Folklore_act_2.jpg; p. 24 https://upload.wikimedia.org/wikipedia/commons/a/a3/Aaron_Dessner_at_Way_Out_West_2014.jpg; p. 25 (Jack Antonoff) Loredana Sangiuliano/Shutterstock.com; p. 25 (Joe Alwyn) lev radin/Shutterstock.com; p. 28 (song lyrics) Ritu Manoj Jethani/Shutterstock.com.

Printed in the United States of America

CPSIA compliance information: Batch #CWGS25: For further information contact Gareth Stevens at 1-800-542-2595.

CONTENTS

BOLDFACE WORDS APPEAR IN THE GLOSSARY.

SONGWRITER, STORYTELLER

Taylor Swift is a huge music star. She's also a prolific songwriter who has written or co-written all of her songs. Taylor has been praised as one of the best songwriters of our time!

Taylor's music has changed over time from country to pop, to songs with sounds of rock, hip-hop, and folk. What ties all of it together is Taylor's lyrics, or the words to her songs; the stories she tells through her songs; and the way the songs connect with her fans.

KNOW-IT-ALL

Prolific means having made a lot of something. Taylor has written hundreds of songs—and likely even more fans have never heard!

Country star Keith Urban once said: "A good songwriter can have you see the flowers in a song. A great songwriter can have you see and feel them. But a truly gifted songwriter's song will have you see, feel, and smell those roses in the window. That's Taylor."

WRITING HER OWN SONGS

By 11 years old, Taylor had visited Nashville, Tennessee, trying to get a record deal. People in the country music industry, or business, didn't sign her then. So, Taylor tried harder by writing her own songs and learning to play guitar. Taylor signed her first songwriting deal at 13. Her family moved close to Nashville around then too.

Not long after, Taylor met songwriter Liz Rose. They started writing together weekly. Taylor brought song ideas to their meetings, and Liz helped her edit and shape them. One of their early **collaborations** resulted in Taylor's first single, "Tim McGraw."

LIZ ROSE

Taylor was just 16 when her first album, *Taylor Swift*, came out in 2006. She has writing credits on every song on the album! This means she is named as a songwriter.

KNOW-IT-ALL

Taylor spent hours a day practicing the guitar and writing songs by the time she was 12.

SOME QUESTIONS

Taylor and Liz wrote a lot of Taylor's early hits together, including "White Horse" on Taylor's second album *Fearless* (2008). But as Taylor won **awards** for *Fearless*, questions kept coming up: Just how much of the songwriting was Taylor's and how much did co-writers like Liz write?

In response, Taylor wrote *Speak Now* (2010), an album on which she had no co-writers on the standard version, or form, of the album. It was written over two years in "real time," meaning Taylor wrote the songs as things happened in her life.

KNOW IT ALL

In 2009, Taylor won an MTV Video Music Award. Rapper Kanye West interrupted her speech, sparking a long-lasting public struggle between them. Taylor wrote "Innocent" on *Speak Now* about it.

Fans and the press tried to figure out who songs on *Speak Now* were about, calling out former boyfriends of Taylor's like Joe Jonas and John Mayer.

THIS THING WAS A MASTERPIECE

Speak Now's success mostly silenced Taylor's **critics** who didn't think she really wrote her songs. Some of Taylor's most beloved music—and biggest hits to that point—came out on *Red* in 2012. *Rolling Stone* wrote in 2021 that *Red* showed Taylor was the not just the best "pop songwriter of her **generation**, but one of the all-timers."

How does she do it? Taylor has said that she writes songs in the same "uncomplicated," or simple, way she did as a kid writing in her room.

KNOW IT ALL

Taylor has written songs for other artists too, including "Better Man" for Little Big Town!

THE RED TOUR, 2013

During The Eras Tour (2023–2024), Taylor performed songs from *Red*. Her costume called to mind the costume she wore on The Red Tour 10 years earlier!

RED ERA SET, THE ERAS TOUR, 2023

MAKING OF A SONG

Taylor writes all the time. She keeps voice memos, or notes, in her phone of good lines she comes up with. The song "Blank Space" from *1989* (2014) was a combination, or mix, of many of the best lines she had written over the years! Taylor keeps a list of words she likes too.

That's how a song can start for Taylor, from a line or cool word. They also come from **experiences** in Taylor's life. Writing helps her work through her feelings.

Taylor says she likes to take common phrases, or groups of words, and twist them a bit when writing lyrics. Here are just a few examples paired with the common phrase Taylor is twisting and its meaning.

TAYLOR'S TURN OF PHRASE

COMMON PHRASE:
something old, something new, something borrowed, and something blue

MEANING:
Brides commonly carry an old, new, borrowed, and blue item for luck at their wedding.

COMMON PHRASE:
All's well that ends well.

MEANING:
If the ending is happy, the hurt leading up to it is okay.

TAYLOR'S LYRICS:
My heart's been borrowed and yours has been blue / All's well that ends well to end up with you.
("Lover," *Lover*)

COMMON PHRASE:
With age comes wisdom.

MEANING:
The older you get, the more knowledge you gain.

TAYLOR'S LYRICS:
I have this thing where I get older but just never wiser.
("Anti-Hero," *Midnights*)

COMMON PHRASE:
People who live in glass houses shouldn't throw stones.

MEANING:
Don't call out other people's flaws when you aren't perfect either.

TAYLOR'S LYRICS:
Baby I could build a castle out of all the bricks they threw at me.
("New Romantics," *1989*)

COMMON PHRASE:
You're the man!

MEANING:
You're the best.

TAYLOR'S LYRICS:
I'm so sick of them coming at me again / 'cause if I was a man / then I'd be the man.
("The Man," *Lover*)

COMMON PHRASE:
Go with grace.

MEANING:
Leave a situation with a calm manner.

TAYLOR'S LYRICS:
I didn't have it in myself to go with grace / 'Cause when I'd fight, you used to tell me I was brave.
("My Tears Ricochet," *folklore*)

Taylor is never far from a piano or guitar and may start writing a melody, or tune, right when a good line comes to her. This is how the song "Lover" came about. Taylor wrote the first line of it when in bed at night and then headed to the piano to write more.

Taylor uses common song parts, including verses, a chorus, and a bridge, in each song. These parts keep her ideas organized, or orderly, and help the listener follow and sing along.

KNOW IT ALL

Verses are the parts of a song that tell much of the story. A chorus is the part that repeats. The bridge connects two parts of the song, such as a verse and chorus, and may introduce a new melody.

Taylor says she sometimes writes for hours at a time when she's feeling hopeful about a song she's working on.

IN TAYLOR'S WORDS

"A lot of songwriting is things you learn ... and knowing how to craft a song. But there are **mystical**, magical moments ... when an idea that is fully formed just pops into your head."
(*Harpar's Bazaar*, July 10, 2018)

LOVE STORIES

Taylor may be best known for her songs about love. She has written about all the parts of love:

- meeting someone new: "Enchanted"
- loving a friend: "You Belong With Me"
- falling in love: "Treacherous"
- being in love: "New Year's Day"
- how love ended: "So Long, London"
- heartbreak: "Last Kiss"

Starting with *Speak Now* and *Red*, the public tried to figure out the **relationships** that sparked each song. In 2024, lists of the songs from her album *The Tortured Poets Department (TTPD)* paired with reasons why certain songs are about one person or another were shared for weeks.

Taylor started dating football player Travis Kelce around 2023. Fans guess that "The Alchemy" on *TTPD* is about him. There are lyrics that seem to be about Travis winning the Super Bowl in 2024.

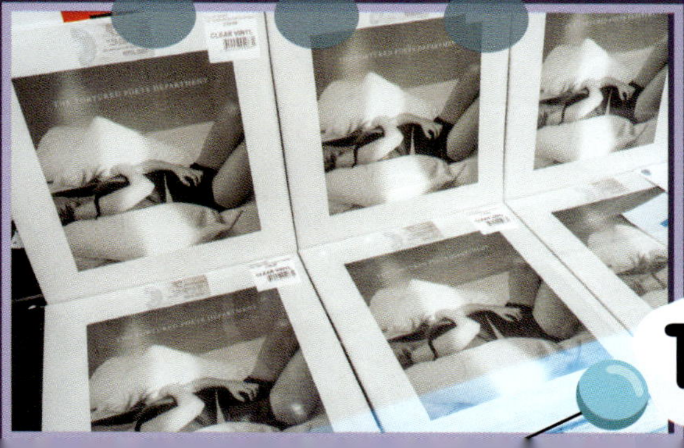

IN TAYLOR'S WORDS

"When it comes to my songwriting and my life, they are one in the same."
(*Nashville Songwriter Awards*, 2022)

POETRY IN SONG

Taylor's songs connect with fans because of universal, or common, feelings in them. Many fans feel her best songs use **details**—such as the scarf in "All Too Well"—to make the song's story feel personal.

Taylor uses imagery to bring the song's story to life. In "Maroon," she sings about "laughing with my feet in your lap." The chorus of "You're On Your Own, Kid" starts with "sprinkler splashes and fireplace ashes." This line has both imagery and **rhyme**, which Taylor also uses a lot!

KNOW-IT-ALL

Imagery is the way a writer uses words to make images, or pictures, the reader or listener can see in their mind.

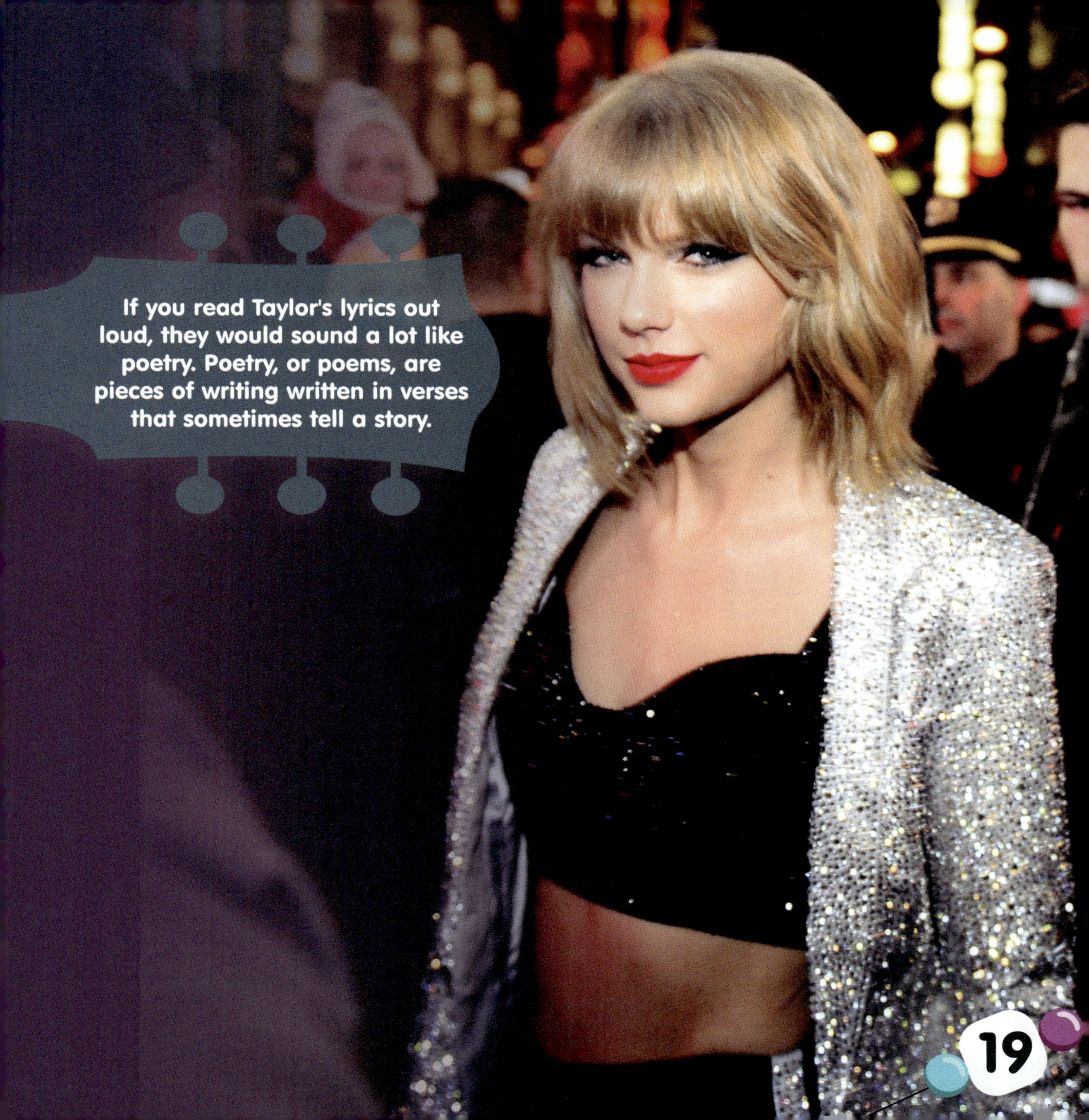

If you read Taylor's lyrics out loud, they would sound a lot like poetry. Poetry, or poems, are pieces of writing written in verses that sometimes tell a story.

A MESSAGE TO THE HATERS

From "Mean" to "thanK you aIMee," Taylor has written songs directed at haters, or those who criticize her loudly and openly, for many years. "This Is Why We Can't Have Nice Things" likely tells of her problems with Kanye West. Parts of "You Need to Calm Down" address those who stand against the **LGBTQ+** community.

In 2019, Taylor was asked why she keeps singing to the haters. She replied: "When they stop coming to me, I will stop singing to them."

KNOW IT ALL

Taylor has also sung about how hard it can be in the spotlight. In the song "You're on Your Own, Kid," Taylor sings: "I gave my blood, sweat, and tears for this."

Some songs on Taylor's first totally pop album, *1989*, were about having fun with friends. Her "girl squad" has included other famous faces like Selena Gomez.

THEN IT CHANGED

When the COVID-19 **pandemic** hit in 2020, Taylor had to cancel many concerts. Later that year, she put out two albums: *folklore* and *evermore*. Both were full of imagery and had quieter musical arrangements. They put Taylor's songwriting on full display.

Writing these albums changed how Taylor wrote songs a bit. She got away from writing only about her life and love. She made up characters and their feelings and stories. Taylor said it made her feel good to write this way!

KNOW-IT-ALL

Folklore and *evermore* were Taylor's first albums with songs marked with an E for "explicit." This means they have adult language in them.

IN TAYLOR'S WORDS

"I was so happy that my world felt opened up creatively. There was a point ... that I got to as a writer who only wrote very **diaristic** songs that I felt it was **unsustainable**."
(Apple Music interview, December 15, 2020)

Taylor has won the Grammy Award for album of the year four times—one of those wins was for *folklore*.

A LITTLE HELP FROM HER FRIENDS

Taylor is a hardworking songwriter on her own. Still, she often works with collaborators on her music. Sometimes these people are just co-writers. Others have written with her and produced her music, which means they guide and oversee a song or album.

AARON DESSNER

"cardigan"
"seven"
"the last great american dynasty"
"But Daddy I Love Him"
"So High School"
"Clara Bow"

JACK ANTONOFF

"Out of the Woods"
"Look What You Made Me Do"
"Cruel Summer"
"august"
"Anti-Hero"

MAX MARTIN

"I Knew You Were Trouble"
"Blank Space"
"Shake It Off"
"Delicate"

WILLIAM BOWERY (JOE ALWYN)

"betty"
"champagne problems"
"Sweet Nothing"

LIZ ROSE

"Tim McGraw"
"Teardrops on My Guitar"
"You Belong with Me"
"White Horse"
"All Too Well"

These are some of Taylor's most important collaborators and some of the songs they have co-written with her.

REMAKING HER MASTERS

Taylor began a special project around 2020. She began rerecording her first albums to own the master recordings of these albums. Masters are the official, original recordings of music. She added "Taylor's Version" to the title of each rerecording. Each included songs that didn't make the original album, a present for fans who listened to or bought the new versions.

Taylor's songwriting has connected with fans of all ages worldwide. There's no question that the stories and poetry of her lyrics have been part of making her a superstar!

IN TAYLOR'S WORDS

"Writing songs is my life's work."
(*Nashville Songwriter Awards*, 2022)

TAYLOR'S ALBUMS

2006 Taylor Swift

2008 FEARLESS

2010 Speak Now

2012 RED

2014 1989

2017 reputation

2019 Lover

2020 folklore and evermore

2021 FEARLESS *(Taylor's Version)* and RED *(Taylor's Version)*

2022 Midnights

2023 Speak Now *(Taylor's Version)* and 1989 *(Taylor's Version)*

2024 THE TORTURED POETS DEPARTMENT and THE TORTURED POETS DEPARTMENT: THE ANTHOLOGY

As a credited writer on her first six albums, Taylor has publishing rights. That means she can record the songs again after a certain amount of time. That's what she has done with the Taylor's Versions!

ACTIVITY: WRITE YOUR OWN SONG LYRICS

Taylor Swift started writing songs when she was just a kid. You can do it too! You can work by yourself or with a friend or two to write the words to your own song.

MATERIALS

- phone, tablet, or computer that can access the internet
- pen or pencil
- writing paper or notebook

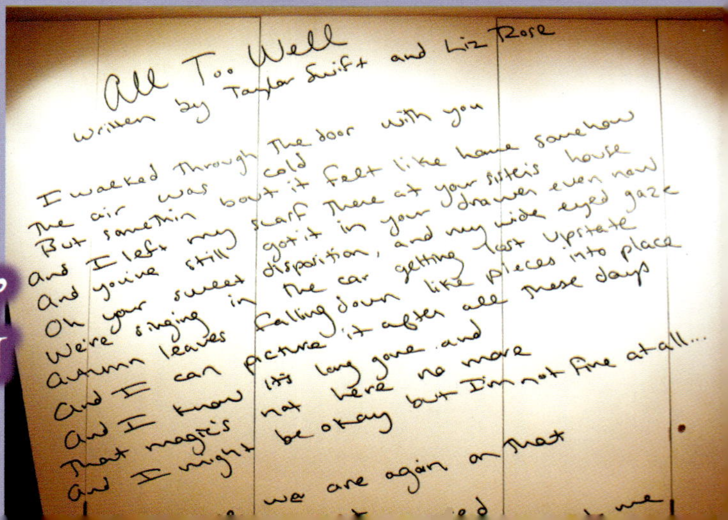
All Too Well
Written by Taylor Swift and Liz Rose

I walked through the door with you
The air was cold
But somethin bout it felt like home somehow
And I left my scarf there at your sister's house
And you've still got it in your drawer even now
Oh your sweet disposition, and my wide eyed gaze
We're singing in the car getting lost Upstate
Autumn leaves falling down like pieces into place
And I can picture it after all these days
And I know it's long gone and
That magic's not here no more
And I might be okay but I'm not fine at all...

"ALL TOO WELL" HANDWRITTEN LYRICS

STEP 1

Get some ideas! With the permission of your caregiver, look up lyrics to some of your favorite songs. Ask yourself:

- What do you like about them?
- How do they make you feel?
- What do they make you think about?

STEP 2

Next, consider the words and word order of the lyrics.

- Do any of the words rhyme?
- Are there any interesting words that stand out to you?
- Is there any imagery?
- Does the song have a certain structure, such as verse, chorus, verse, bridge, chorus?

STEP 3

Write down your ideas. They can be about how you feel about another person or about something that has happened in your life. They can tell how the beach looks on the perfect summer day. Be creative! There is no wrong way to begin.

STEP 4

Write a few lines. Then, read them out loud. What can you change to make them sound better? What details can you add to make a picture with your words? Keep going with this until you have several lines that go together.

STEP 5

Consider using a song form like the one in step 2 to help you organize your thoughts. What are you missing to make the story make sense or get your idea across? Keep going back and updating your work as you go.

BONUS: Add music! Do you play an instrument or have a friend who does? You can write your own special melody to go with your lyrics!

GLOSSARY

award: A prize given for doing something.

collaboration: Work with another person to make something. One person who works with another is a collaborator.

critic: A person whose job it is to judge the arts, such as music. Also, someone who criticizes another person. To criticize means to talk about the problems with something.

detail: A small part of something.

diaristic: Being like a diary, or a notebook in which someone writes their thoughts and feelings.

experience: Something that a person has done or that has happened to a person.

generation: A group of individuals born about the same time.

LGBTQ+: Stands for the lesbian, gay, bisexual, transgender, and queer or questioning community.

mystical: Having to do with having a meaning or spiritual connection that is hard to see or understand.

pandemic: A time in which an illness spreads quickly and affects a large area of the world.

relationship: A connection to another person, including one of love.

rhyme: The ending sound shared by two or more words or phrases.

unsustainable: Not able to last for a long time.

FOR MORE INFORMATION

Books

Burk, Rachelle. *The Story of Taylor Swift: An Inspiring Biography for Young Readers*. Naperville, IL: Callisto Publishing, 2024.

Gottlieb, Beth. *Taylor Swift*. Buffalo, NY: Enslow Publishing, 2024.

Websites

Taylor Swift
www.taylorswift.com/
Keep up with Taylor on her official website.

Taylor Swift: Artist
www.grammy.com/artists/taylor-swift/15450
Find out more about the Grammy Awards Taylor has been nominated for and won.

Publisher's note to educators and parents: Our editors have carefully reviewed these websites to ensure that they are suitable for students. Many websites change frequently, however, and we cannot guarantee that a site's future contents will continue to meet our high standards of quality and educational value. Be advised that students should be closely supervised whenever they access the internet.

INDEX